FIND G(

FIND GOLDIE

BRIAN DUGGAN

To order additional copies of this book, contact:
Xlibris
800-056-3182
www.Xlibrispublishing.co.uk
Orders@Xlibrispublishing.co.uk
790191

I wanted to thank some people, I'd like to thank Bob, Bernie, Dave, John, Caroline, Audrey and Jill.

The staff of Tallaght Hospital, Michelle and Emma and to all the ones who helped along the way.

This book is dedicated to
the memory of
Miriam Nicholson.

GOLDIES ODYSSEY

BY

B DUGGAN

IT WAS A lovely day when Goldie ran away. But it turned out to be such a turn of events for us and for Goldie.

Hi there I'm Goldie's owner. Well one of them anyway. There's me, my wife, my son, Goldie and James. James is our other dog. We had just come back from a short few days away, same as we did every year. This one was no different. When we'd go away my brother-in-law would look after Goldie and James until we came back. When we'd get back Goldie and James would be so excited to see us. I'd usually take James for a long walk. Goldie didn't like the long walks so it would be just me and James.

When we got back my wife went to visit her father in hospital. We stayed home, the rest of us, no different than we always did. Our fridge, I remember, had just broke so got about emptying the ruined stuff out to get ready for the new one. So I started throwing all that in the outside bin, as you do. I did that a few times then shut the front door and started doing something else, Then I sat down to wait for me other half's return. But something was wrong; Goldie wasn't there. Where was she? I shouted up to my son, "is Goldie up there", "no dad she's not" came the reply. So I checked all the rooms in the house, under the beds, everywhere. No sign. I started to panic a bit. So I called my lads nanny on the phone to see if she could watch my son while I went out to look for Goldie around the road where we live. Goldie can't be gone far ehh. My son is autistic so he cannot be left alone, luckily his nanny was in so I dropped him off at her house and got on my bike to go look for Goldie. I thought it was very strange because Goldie never did anything like this before. We've had her four years so what a surprise this was. I looked all over the road and knocked on a few doors, no one had seen her. Things were beginning to get hairy now. I rang my wife to tell her but her phone was off. I looked all over my estate for the next hour or so but no sign. It was starting to get dark and I started to get this really bad feeling in my stomach. I called her name all along but there was no sign.

My wife had come back home by now and she could not believe what I was telling her - Goldie had done a runner. I live in Finglas by the way, on the north side of Dublin. I'm telling you this for a reason that will become clear as we go along. It was pitch dark by now so I had to stop. I called the police to let them know of Goldie's disappearance just in case somebody handed her in. We'll find her in the morning I told myself.

I couldn't sleep that night just thinking of her out there. I kept saying she can't be far; she's probably only a few doors away - but little did I know that this was the just the start. This was the beginning of Goldie's Odyssey.

The next day was Sunday so I had lots of time to search. I walked around the corner and I met a man who said he had seen a dog this morning running into the factories just around the same time as Goldie went missing. This has to be her. So I called the security and set about looking all through the factories and the surrounding roads. My wife did the same whenever she could as she had to stay at home mostly to mind our son because he has special needs so he has to be looked after all the time. So really it was up to me. My son really started to miss Goldie by now. She is part of his day and he hates changes. Especially a change like this. It went on like this for the rest of the day so we decided to put it up on facebook in order to create awareness among the public. We put the only picture of Goldie that we had up on the Facebook page and hoped for the best, Just then someone said they had seen her that day on Griffith Avenue, Damn, I thought, I've been looking in the wrong area. A chap said he saw her down by the Scout Den so I headed down there straight away. I got in touch with this lad who said she was there earlier but had moved off. "Which way" says I? So I picked up the pace on me bike and cycled all over Griffith Park, Moby Road, Phibsboro Avenue, anywhere and everywhere.

The next day we got a call to say she was seen on Brian Road, my namesake - a bit of luck maybe. Brian Road is just across from Phibsboro Ave and across from Fairview park, in behind the shops. More people joined the search. We got a photographic sighting of her in transit at this point so we knew for definite she was in this area. The trouble was she was hiding. She was scared and anytime anyone would approach her she would bolt. We plastered the place in posters and then one of the girls who was helping set up the "Find Goldie" Facebook page. This was going to help no end. This is what we needed.

By now I was starting to realise the size of the area we had to find her. It was big, especially in dog terms. Every day we asked people and more joined in. Friends and strangers, (who aren't strangers anymore), gave up their time to help. Although we hadn't found her yet it felt good that all these people were keeping their eyes peeled in helping to bring Goldie home. I started keeping an eye on the Pounds just in case she turned up in one of them. Not nice to have to go up and see all those poor dogs who end up there, it's like doggie prison. But let's not go into all that - you get the picture.

Now Goldie is her name because she is just that; golden in colour and small, that's how I would describe her. She has a black face, white paw and is only about a foot off the ground.

She's fast though,very fast. Sometimes people thought she was a fox. I had all sorts of false alarms during the search, in the sense that when people read the description it transpired that a lot of dogs start to look like Goldie. But that didn't matter, all leads had to be checked. But each time you build yourself up to be let down constantly. It's no ones fault, they're just following they're nose I suppose and trying to help. Another thing that kept happening was I'd leave an area and as soon as I was home Goldie would pop up, someone would see her - and then she'd be gone again. Where was she sleeping? That's what I was trying to sus out, If we knew that we could get her.

When a dog runs away they seem to run in circles like one minute we'd be in Fairvew then minutes later up on Gracepark Road, Collins Ave, Malahide Road, Moby Road, Drumcondra and back to Fairview. Even in the rain. If we were at one end of the road she'd be at the other, like Murphys Law. That's how it went. Frustrating. Hard to reach.

Even the cops were getting involved. Sometimes I'd get calls from them. This went on in these areas for about 2 weeks when we got a call from a girl to say she was seen in the bushes on Griffith Parade and also in the Carers Centre. She was seen looking in the bins so I quickly headed around there and showed the security guy a picture. He said "yes without a doubt this dog is here" so I hung around for a bit. I remember it was spilling rain so I said there is no way she is out in this, too cute she is. So I went home and said to my wife "I'll go there early in the morning and see can I catch her sleeping". So I did. The next morning was really sunny so I jumped on me bike and went down to look. Once I was there I peered into the bushes where she was seen but nothing. I asked around and nothing. I checked all that day and nothing. She had moved on again. We got a call later to say she was seen on Shalmartin Road, which is just down the road, a big long road which leads back to Brian Road. Here it was like a big joke at this stage. I mean Goldie runs from Brian's house and ends up on Brian Road - I don't know. She must have been so afraid out there what with cars flying by all the time and everywhere is strange. How was she doin' it? How was she surviving? i think she was goin out at night and hiding during the day, it was quiet at night time, under the cover of darkness. We always had to wind the search down around twelve as I had work in the mornings. I'd go home every night wondering where she was sleeping and hope that maybe, just maybe she'd be at the front door the next morning.

By now she was getting further out of reach. Someone had seen her going into every house on a road close to Fairview which made us sad because we knew she was looking for her door, her familiar place and couldn't find it. How sad is that?

Around this time we got a call to say she was seen flying across Fairview Road into the park. Now that's a dangerous road with 6 lanes of fast moving traffic. But she made it across. We began to think that now she was in the park maybe this was good open spaces and that, but then she was seen heading back to Marino. She's some dog for one dog! I mean I didn't teach her to cross the road but she seemed like a seasoned pro! Dog wide that's what i say! Or else she was getting a lift.

She always seemed to be just a couple of steps ahead of us, If I wasn't on me bike I was in my friend's car or on the bus, But remember dogs can go all the places we can't and you nearly have to start thinking like a dog yourself - where would I go if I were Goldie? But we were determined to get her. You can't give up on your family, that's what she is she's family. She has her own chair and her own space, I keep my dogs in the house so she was used to a bit of comfort. I wonder how she was at night, did she think of home? I thought of her under the moon and stars, either way she was a survivor and I wasn't giving up. Things were about to change, it was about to get a little harder.

By now she had been seen in Drumcondra, Dorset Street, Fairview and back to Marino. If we could keep her in these areas we should be able to grab her, or someone should. But every time people got anywhere near her she'd bolt. She wasn't used to other people and she had a very nervous disposition. I suppose you would be out there in this strange environment. It was nearly like someone took her put her in their car and let her out, just for a laugh. Or, she thought she was in trouble and hid. I imagined her in the bushes at times looking out saying "you won't catch me" but then other times she would be missing home. All the nice treats she would be missing out on and all the presses she had to raid with her ole pal James.

One day we got a call to say she was seen running really fast down East Wall Road,and over by Lidl in East Wall. It seemed now she was moving further away. I took off on my bike and headed over there straight away with a few friends. We littered the place with posters of Goldie and asked as many people as possible if they had seen her. Some people said they had seen her but said they hadn't a hope of catching her. Ask yourself, have you ever tried to grab a small wiry dog in transit? Well good luck with that, it's almost impossible. I knew if I could just get close to her she would know me straight away. Sure she's been looking for her place franticly since she ran off. Of course, we got the usual prank calls also. At this point someone rang to say they had her in Lidl at East Wall. So my friend and I drove down and I went in. I kind of realised there is no way Goldie is in here but I gave it the benefit of the doubt and asked the security guy who was Polish. Of course he hadn't a clue what I was talking about. I walked off and rang the number back of the reportee and his dad answered and shouted "there's no lost dogs here only meself". I said "fine" and cursed the time wasters.

So while we were there we investigated Alexandra Road, down the docks. Now this place is a city in itself. I put up some posters and asked security did they see Goldie, but to no avail. We drove around for a while, no sign of her. I said to myself if she's in here we haven't got much hope of spotting her, it's like a needle in a haystack.

We went home with the usual feelings of where could she be? Is she hungry? Is she injured? Is she scared? Is she missing us? "Keep the faith" I told myself. I had to. We spent the next few days searching East Wall and then all the other places that she was spotted in on the way back, you always have to check all those other places in case she doubles back, which they do. She always seems to do a wide circle everywhere she goes, so it gets harder the longer she is out there.

A week or so passed and then we got a call from a man who spotted her running across the road from Sheriff Street, past The Point and over into the lorry area of the docks. Now that's one dangerous road! I mean for a dog who is terrified of traffic. At home she used to duck down when cars went past on our short walks. But it seemed she was navigating her way around ok at this point. So over I went and the man in the Goods In and Out area said he would take my number and a picture of Goldie and call me as soon as he see's anything. That's all I could do for now.

I have to say most people were very helpful when they heard of a small dog who had gone missing. You get to see first hand who's helpful and who isn't. Most are great. Most people have their own dog anyway.

I remember hanging around that area down at the docks. I thought to myself if Goldie goes down that dual carriageway it's curtains for her because that leads to the Dublin port tunnel. I would come here with the song Homeward Bound playing in my head and thinking of her trying to find her way home, mind you if she went through the tunnel she would end up almost back home!

And then I could see a cruise ship had docked. I remember the Goods In & Out man had told me that sometimes animals get into the containers and get shipped out to other countries. Imagine Goldie the Seafarer, heading out on the Star of the Sea cruise ship with her paws up having a cocktail or a dogtail, saying to herself "to hell with them I'm off to find new horizons"! Her and a few pals maybe.going to Holland, or even jumping into a lorry and heading off on a long distance road trip and then the driver taking a shine to her and keeping her. I said if that be so well I would be happy to know someone looked after her and gave her a nice home.

Then there were times when horrible thoughts came into my head about things that could happen. I would force those thoughts out, I won't think like that. I can't. I watched the Facebook Page every day and got in contact with Dublin Port staff, but there had been no other sighting of Goldie. I was losing hope now, one week then two weeks with no sign. Not one sighting. Considering we has sightings everyday, now none, I resigned myself to the fact that she was gone.

Somebody had her. No dogs home had her, no one came across with any news. It looked very bad and we were losing momentum.

What could we do next? I walked home slowly some nights, clear nights with only the moon and stars for company. That's how I imagined Goldie, sitting somewhere looking out at the stillness of the night, wondering how to get home. I heard through all this that dogs don't do that they just get on with it. Finding food is probably her only motivation. Weeks went by and on into the second month and she had all but disappeared. Where could she be? Did she get that ship by any chance? Where would she go next? I thought of her trapped in Dublin Port going around in circles, frantic, or maybe she might come back with sand on her paws from holidays abroad, I just had to keep the faith. I wasn't goin to allow myself to think of her in trouble until I got news of that.

It was a rainy Sunday I remember and I got a call. It was Store Street Garda Station to say they think they found Goldie. They had found a dog; female, tan, white tipped paws and black muzzle face. "Thats her" I said. They had her in a kennel there so I was leaping around with the news that this was her. Then hold on maybe not, say nothing till we see. So in I went with her picture. When I got there the guard brought me around to the kennels which were decent enough digs for arrested dogs. Goldie the Fugitive. Goldie the Gangster. Goldie [Bullet Legs] Duggan. This was her new persona now. As we got to the kennel we looked and she was gone. What? No way! Escape from Store Street, Goldie? What is this? The Garda called her co-worker and he said someone had brought this dog for a walk. I said "that's the last thing she needs after walking the legs off herself". The Garda asked me if I'd mind waiting to see, "of course not" says I. But just as a matter of interest is it a big or small dog? Big she said........why didn't I ask that over the phone? So that was that. Wrong answer. My heart sank again. So I waited anyway just to see what this dog looked like. Next thing in walked a big tan Great Dane. No way this dog here would have swallowed Goldie whole. I laughed me head off on the way home. I suppose it wasn't their fault, they were only goin on the description. Goldie, tan coloured, white tipped paws and black muzzle face. Just the wrong height and weight. That one was the Mike Tyson Goldie. So here we were, back to where we were before THE PORT.

Imagine if she did,imagine if she took off somewhere abroad,Hm, she said,I wonder which container will I go into,just for the night,to get in out of the cold like.lets have a little peak in here.She chose the one with all the bikes in it.hey that looks like brians bike,you know my owner, thats the one he always goes around on.I wonder where he is,thought I saw him the other day,almost certain I heard him? That night goldie settled in for a nice sleep in this container in Dublin docks,and as she slipped into a comfy sleep with the sound of the boat and ship horns in the distance of the night,the door shut on the container and she never heard a sound.Not even the sound of the lock and seels going on.This container was ready for shipping and nobody knows that goldie is in there. The next morning with the hustle and bustle and clanking and banging of all the containers getting shipped goldie awoke to feel like she was floating in the air.Wow she said, as her container sailed through the air as it was been picked up by the crane,she could just about see out a crack in the door. She started to bark loudly and jump of the door but nobody could hear.The container plonked down with a thud,and when it settled she could see she was about 100 foot up from the floor,the floor of a big cargo ship heading to god only knows where? She turned around to face the darkness of the container,turned around and sat peering out the gap in the door.All was quiet.Then all of a sudden there was a load whistle and a long sound of the horn,and before you could say, all aboard,she was pulling away from the shipyard and heading out to sea.She could feel that butterfly feeling of fear and sat there in the big unknown future that she was about to imbark on.Where were we going? Whats going to happen to me? Where is my owner? why hasn't he come.In the distance just as land was about to disappear she could see a figure on the shore on a black bike looking out across the sea,kind of looks like my owner.she decided there was noting else she could do so she closed her eyes and took a nap,it was so quiet except for the sea gulls crying. It was a nice feeling floating on the sea,she never felt this before.so she dreamt away there dreaming of home and james and big lovely hunks of meat and chicken and all manner of food and treats of course.She awoke to the container shaking violently and it was quiet chilly,she looked out the gap it was a storm a huge blowy storm up went the container and down with a crash hold on, hold on.She held on to one of the bikes for dear life.this was the rockiest ride she was ever on worse then been washed in the bath.How long was this going to last? I hope not too long. Just then it was all calm again just like that.She peared out the gap in the door and she could see land again she could see a little coloured flag blowing in the distance it was red,and white and blue,she was heading to Britain. I wonder what that's going to be like?The ship came into a bustling ship yard just like the one she left back there in Ireland,and before she knew it she was being picked up again with another big crane and with a big thud the container came to a holt.all people were talking outside sounding a bit different then what she was used to.sounds like Oi and watch that mate.but no one was opening her container just chattering outside. So she sat put and just listened.just then the door opened and a big flash of light blinded her so she couldn't see this big hand coming down to grab her.Oi what you doing in there hey john it's a dog. nice isn't she.Where did you come from.Hey lets get you out of there. The man brought her into this big room there was a real oily smell all around,then there was a huge big plate put down and all manner of meat was put down onto it. yes yes just like I dreamt it,she tucked into a big feed of fish and steak pieces and lovely jelly and a huge big bone for after.This is more like it I couldn't find any of this back in Ireland mind you I did back in my house though.This was the best feed ive had in ages.

After the big dinner she sat down for a nap. she felt a little bit safer in this place,a bit noisy but not too bad.The men were chatting away and I think they said something like,when are you heading back to Ireland?in about days ive to head over to Europe for a bit.hey il take our new furry friend with me and I can bring her it is a her isn't it?yes john shes a she alright.yeah I,l be heading back over to Ireland after that so I can bring her straight back next Saturday.Ok john you take her along.

Next morning after breakfast of another big plate of assorted meat, john carried her into his big cab and she took her seat next to him for the journey.After a big see yea later we were of.Of on another big adventure,they were heading to dover,bringing a load of stuff with them and on to Calais,wow what a time im going to have.

They were heading up to another ship yard but this one was a sail through one.this time we drove straight on to this big ship I was made to hide again in the cab,because im so small that's what I did I kept down till we got out of the way of everyone,I decided to have a sleep till we got there.the weather was good and I felt safe here. As soon as we got out of another ship yard we were on the road.france,a different country,wonder what the grubs like over here,before I knew it I had that answered. A nice bit of meat but this time it was a bit sweet and it looked like a big long sausage.not bad not bad at all.Everything looked a lot bigger over here.I heard himself say we wouldn't be long here maybe a day or two,then back to Ireland.Lets enjoy it anyway.We were rolling into paris,A few sights to see here,the arc de triumph, the eifel tower,and my favorite of course euro Disney.I met a few other dogs here but they were a bit difficult to under stand,but we still had our own ways so I still knew what was going on.We done our delivery and left off the big container,and chilled out for the night. Before I turned in for the night,john took out a huge big bone,this was heaven.I got to see a good bit of the world here.But at the same time we were heading back tomorrow,and I really hope my owner will come and get me im sure he will.

We woke the next morning and I must have slept in because we were already on the sea heading back home. I had a great time and I got to taste a few different tastes from some different places.I over heard john say that when we get back there going to send me to the pound.well im not going there,im going to do a runner as soon as I get back.we drove straight off the ship as soon as we got back. when we stopped and john opened the door I jumped out and did a runner up a few familiar streets, bye john it was great,but im on the run again hopping to be found.

Around this time I stuck a few posters over the bridge that leads to the southside. If Goldie takes this direction she would be heading to Ringsend/Irishtown direction. Two weeks had passed now without a sign. We were in for a surprise though because as soon as we got to this point Goldie was about to stick her head up.

I was sitting down one Friday evening when we got a call to say they just seen Goldie flying down the middle of the road just along Portabello Bridge, which is on Dublin's south side. So I jumped up on the bike and tore into town as quick as I could; if I could get over quick enough we might have a chance of getting her. But alas, not a chance. So I cycled the length and breadth of the canal area searching. I remember it was a Friday night and one of the girls who was a big part in this story was about to come into play - someone who would lead me to another lady who would be a huge part in this story. I asked a heap of people along the canal if they had seen Goldie, but no sightings. By now of course it was getting dark so I had to give it up again and wait till the next day. On the way home I felt like hey she survived all of that, she overcame all the obstacles of the main road along Rathmines and she was bedding down somewhere now, we have to be able to get a hold of her, she's getting used to the way things are so I felt like there was plenty of hope. So she never bothered with the trip abroad after all. She was still in Dublin, mind you she could maybe hop on a barge and head up to Shannon, that would be a long cycle for me.

We started putting up posters all over the surrounding areas,and set up the Find Goldie page. A very kind lady set that up officially and this is how we were able to drum up a lot of real interest. We covered Rathmines, Harolds Cross, ranelagh, Terenure, up and down Kimmage Road. and Bushy Park. The Facebook Page really worked out great because after every sighting you could see the area Goldie had been and calculate where she might be heading. Everyday she was seen, but with a slight difference. She started coming out at night and early morning. This was very hard because when we got a call from anyone it could be at one in the morning. This was when other people who lived in these areas and would in contact with each other. It was like a little network of people giving up their nights and getting out and sometimes even chasing her through housing estates. I remember getting reports from taxi drivers saying they seen this little brown bullet fly by them in the night. Then they would see the posters of her and realise it was her.or other times people would be at bus stops and she would fly by. She covered all area from Churchtown to Kimmage to Crumlin. I was in work one afternoon and one of my work colleagues sawn her on the Bangor Road. Sure I was literally around the corner from there that day so I just missed her by a whisker. She must have been the most looked for dog in the country at this time. She certainly looked the worse for wear at this stage and she had lost a lot of weight.

We filled the place with posters and kept looking as much as we could, and me asking meself the same old questions, where was she sleeping? What was she eating? And most of all how could this little small dog become this little troubadour? She must have walked hundreds of miles by now. Like The Proclaimers song. Well I certainly felt it in my feet but that didn't matter, we had to catch her. If she lasted that long out there chances were we were going to catch up with her, but when? That was the question.

I felt like someone had her and they were letting her out just to wind us up. People were ringing me telling me to ring Chris Barry, Joe Duffy, Ryan Tubridy. I rang them all and sent a message to Tubs but no interest from any them. So it was just our team of people who cared for Goldie.

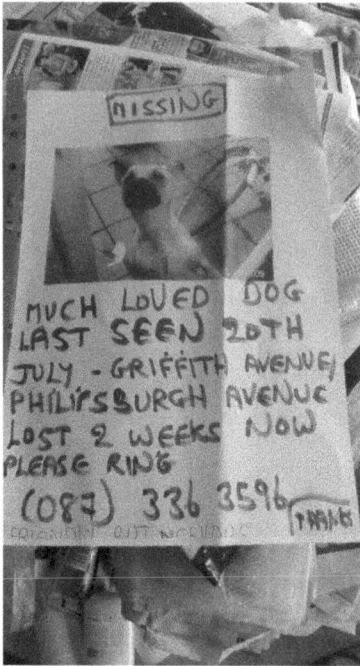

poster of goldie we used for her as lost dog

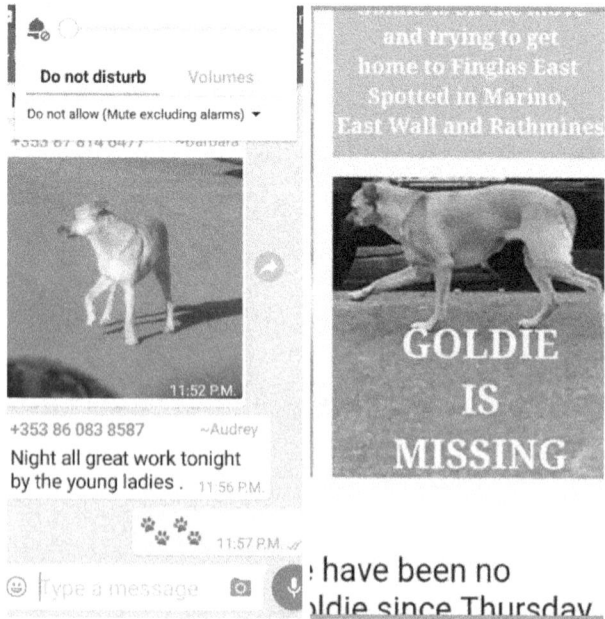

left, goldie tallaght hospital. right, goldie lost

picture taken at night in the hospital carpark. out of reach

she loves to bask in the sunshine.

hiding among the cars, she lived in that carpark for four months

dog on the run

hiding in plain sight

me ringing bob to tell him she came out

bob and bernie, they never let up for a second

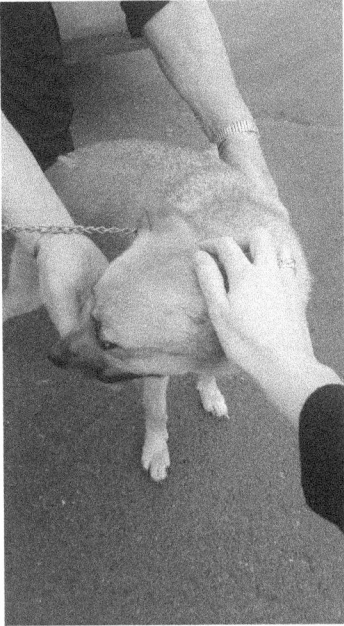

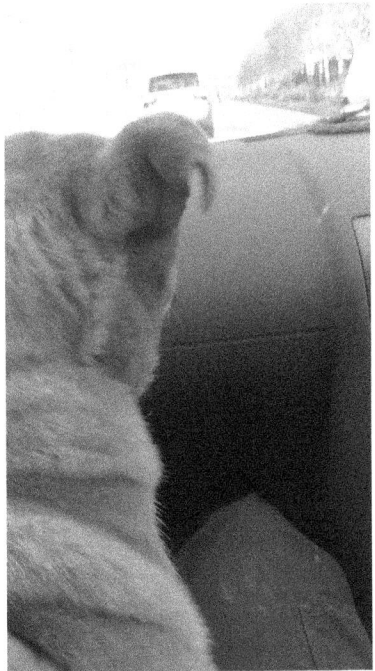

leaving the carpark tallaght hospital, homeward bound

some dog for one dog, back home

It's not easy trying to track or catch a dog. The people who do it are the unsung heros in our lives, they are behind the scenes and we won't notice them until your dog or cat or even birds, imagine, I couldn't believe it when I heard they go after birds as well. Like in a helicopter you would think, but that very thing happened around the time of Goldie goin, no actually when we got her back a girl rang us to ask could we send our man over as she had a bird, I think it was either a budgie or something like that, we get the picture now of course, it injured and frightened one, but the point is that understand how dear our pets are to us. It doesn't matter what the pets are, from snakes to horses, cats and dogs. Hey even a tortoise. Yes we can grow attached to them. I knew a chap when I was growing up who used to bring his tortoise out on a lead, for pure shock value of course for the neighbours. We have a close bond with our pets and when this is broken it's like a family member going missing. But sure who can resist our lovely dogs with their antics and the way they greet us in the mornings and when we come home from wherever. They're delighted to see us and then they grow attached to us too, and if someone invades our space they protect us without hesitation. I have another dog as you know from this story and he is such a character too. James his name is. I remember one evening I used to bring him for his walk up to the local park and each time I let him off the lead he would bolt. No not after anyone, just over to the nearest other dog that was there, just to greet it and have a roll around. Some of the owners didn't like this which lead me to shout his name all over the place; James ….. James …. just to get him back under control Anyway, this particular evening it was just around 6pm, dusk, and of course I looked around and there were no other dogs that I could see except for the one about a half a mile out of the park, you'd need magnifying night time goggles on to see it. So I set James off and away he goes with me calling him back …. James ….. James …. he ignored me and continued over towards the far away dog. As he's approaching the fence I could see a car in the distance. Now I'm on me own here with no one to try to stop James only the roars of me voice, when what does he do but jump the fence and goes straight out onto the road and plonks himself, sheep dog style, on to the middle of the road with the car fast approaching and me trying to reach him and shouting. Too late, the car hit him hindside and James took off mid air and came down on to a sandbank as they were building a couple of houses there. I have a knot in me stomach as I write this. I ran over in a panic and I could hear him crying. But then, to my half panic, half relief, he's still alive but injured. What a relief but also I'm concerned at what injuries he actually has. So, as I'm about to bend down to pick up James the owner of the car comes back crying his eyes out asking is he ok and can I bring him to the vet. Just then, James is up on his feet, not a blemish on him. So as I could see the whole scene unfolding it was plain to see that it wasn't the drivers fault, it was just a pure accident, what. On a dark evening the last thing you're expecting on your journey home from work is a half lab/half collie, jet black in colour, to be lounging around the middle of the road now. But the reaction from that man said it all. He was trying his best to compose himself with the whole thing, he wasn't even concerned about his car, just the dog. There's something in us that does that to us so it's probably that same innate thing that drives the people who spend their lives rescuing animals. We just love the animals. So, off we went t othe vet, I bid farewell to the man first and carried James down with both arms, you know that awkward way way we do, and told the driver not to be worried it wasn't his fault. And James got sorted, no damage, just a very interesting and a little sore flight through the air. And a sore bum of course. He still licks that area even today 8 years later. And he doesn't sit in the middle of any roads.

So, back to Goldie. She was heading up and down along the Dodder River, we could see that now; Churchtown, Perrystown, Old Bawn, back down to Bushy Park, the Dropping Well. I left me jumper down there in case she picked up on me scent, anything was possible.

One Saturday we did an early morning search. We met at the Dropping Well and Rathfarnham, a few of us at one end and a few at the other end. The plan was to meet in the middle and that way we covered all areas. This had to be the ticket I thought to myself, this is it, we're goin to find her today. She was probably hiding in Bushy Park that was my guess. There were so many places to hide, that's what happens when a dog bolts. People always say, sure just call her she'll come back. No I gave up calling at this stage -trap her was what we had to do. As we were about to get started we got a call to say some one has spotted her while they were jogging, only problem was that was in Cheeverstown. What? Sure that's way away, we're miles away from her. One of the lads had an estate car so we threw our bikes in and took off to Cheeverstown. The lady said she saw a dog fitting Goldie's description running up a long straight road, so we got onto this road and there were fences on both sides, no way for her to get through. But no sign of her either. Just then we saw 2 whippets running along side the road, the same colour as Goldie just the wrong breed; a Goldie lookalike. They ran into a halting site so we went in to investigate. We drove around a bit and got a good look at those whippets. The lady made a mistake but that's not suprising because at a glance Goldie looks like a heap of other dogs, but with certain looks that you know straight away when you know her. You know what I mean if you have dogs, you know your own.

So we drove back down to the Dodder area and had another good look around. It was 2 o'clock by now and we had to call it a day. It was a lovely day so I headed down to Sandymont via the Dodder and stuck up some posters. I remember I met a man while I was putting up a poster at a set of traffic lights on Sandymont Road, he said "I saw a dog just like that the other day out there on the sand". "Are you sure?" I said. He said "yip just like that one". And this was the difficulty here, the same looks just a different dog. I sat down for a while thinking mind you my dogs would love it here, but I can't drive so it's not happening. Mind you I said to myself that's one thing I am goin to do I'm goin to learn. But I've got to find Goldie first. I headed back through Irishtown and over towards Fairview via the coastline. By now I was getting a good sense of how she was getting from place to place. I reckoned she was following the rivers, all linking up and then she would wander into whatever area was there. She would then be seen by someone an I'd be alerted to the sighting and by the time I got to the sighting place she would be a few steps ahead of the search all the time.

I went home feeling a little empty but then you brush that off a continue. I must say that by this stage I was kind of enjoying seeing all this side of Dublin. Places I have never really seen. Some really nice spots, places I would never have seen if this trek wasn't happening. We searched all the way through September while the weather was still good and there was still a bit of a stretch in the evenings. The first 2 weeks is nearly always good just in time for the kids to go back to school. That's a bit of the old Irish Murphys Law.

The Facebook page was getting bigger now. People were sharing to their contacts and comments and messages of support were coming in all the time. Conversations over Goldies whereabouts were visible and it was a great platform for me to get some perspective on where Goldie could be by now. Loads of sightings of Goldie were posted to the page; some her, some not. We couldn't seem to pin down her moves too easily now. A few people were convinced she was in Finglas, others said she was still down in the Griffith Road area and some even said she was in Balbriggan. At one point someone even said they had seen her in Cork! Now I know she's good but not that good.

By now we knew she was up around Firhouse. I remember one really nice Sunday I started at Liekiln Park and walked all alongside the river till I got to the Speakers Connolly pub. I got a call from a guy offering to help me promote the Facebook page, he was trying to help with a few ideas. It was around the 2pm mark so I decided to get the bus back to Bushy Park and then head in to see if there was any sign. Just then one of the lads rang to say she was seen up around The Speakers Connolly. What! I just came from there so back on the bus I went and met up with the crew. There was a little house just out on its own, down from The Speaker Connolly's and the lady who lived there said it was definitely Goldie that she saw in her field. We looked, but no sign.

Then we got another call to say she was definitely spotted in a garden down opposite The blue haven pub. Now that was back down the Firhouse Road. My god she was givin us a run for our money. So we investigated that and sure enough the lady living in there said when I showed her a poster that this dog has been coming into her garden and eating the food out of her dogs bowl, So that was it,this was how she was surviving. She was sneaking into gardens and dipping the other doggies food! Good girl Goldie. Also we asked would she mind if we had a look at the entry points in her garden and when we looked low and behold what did it lead to but the Dodder river, right at the back of her garden. Smart girl. All around this time there was sighting after sighting after sighting all along the Dodder and surrounding areas. I remember a man was found dead up around Old Bawn and his boxer dogs ran off. A freind said the cops will probably find Goldie by accident. Yeah but they won't be able to catch her.

I got a call one day and a picture on the page to say she was seen outside the Annunciation Church in Finglas. It definitely looked like her, no collar, same size. The picture was a bit blurred so I raced home to see it, but as usual no sign Later that evening there was a definite sighting of her in Rathfarnham Shopping Centre. So the Finglas sighting was of some other dog, not Goldie.

After this point the trail went quiet. I think the last time she was seen was in a cul- de- sac in Firhouse in the early hours of the morning. This was an impossible situation, I just couldn't be in two places at once and I knew if I could get real close to her she would recognise me and that would be that. But that wasn't to happen.

One day we were in a really upmarket part of Dublin, we were down around Shelbourne Road, Ranelagh, the RDS. It was a lovely Sunday afternoon and I was putting up some posters. I had been asking people if they had seen Goldie around and a few of them said they had but not on this day, just on and off for the last few days. So I spent another day looking and and searching another side of the city that I wasn't used to. The houses around this area were so vast and almost unapproachable, I said to myself "if she gets to find a nice little pad down here she won't want to come home". I could imagine her chillin beside a nice pool or looking out of the top window going "that looks like my owner out there.…… nah it couldn't be, I cannot be sure what would he be doin all the way over here. In any case it is onwards and upwards for me". Could you just imagine it. But I often wondered would she recognise me if she were to turn the corner right now after all it's been 2 and a half months since she left. I suppose to a dog that's a long time but really it wasn't that long.

All the areas we searched have one thing in common — they all have rivers running through them and linking up and leading out to the sea. So I followed all the way out to Sandymount, which in turn lead all the way out to Bray. No this was so so far. I remembered a lady telling me that her dog ran from Ballymun to Bray before they found him and this gave me hope. It also gave me the push to keep on going and never give up. I knew that if I found her it would be really flukey, like that's her out there on the beach or something like that. It was coming towards the evening so I headed back down to Ranelagh and as I was getting to Kennelworth Park I could get the beautiful smell of a BBQ. It turns out there was a hug BBQ in the park. I knew that if Goldie was in this area she'd be here for sure. I looked and looked and got all the more hungry. No way, that was that, no sign. Another day with no luck but with plenty of hope that even if I don't find here today, one day soon I will.

I met up with a couple who helped me when she was in Griffith Avenue, a husband and wife team who spent all that day on the lookout, but with no luck. I saw there were plenty of posters up so her profile was certainly getting raised all along. I thanked them for all their help and headed on home thinking all the while of Goldie, the distinguished dog, the leader of her pack. The boss. This was a different dog and may I say a quite famous dog. That's what was slowly happening here. She was becoming very well known from one end of the city to the other. I felt at this stage she was well able to navigate the city. She had survived this long. And anyway it was becoming a bit of a challenge that I wasn't going to lose, unless the worst happened. So of course I couldn't think like that, so long as she was out there I was goin to find her. I was determined.

It was October now and the dark nights were drawing in and it was getting colder as well. I said if we don't get her soon she's gonna be done for. She was seen up around Tallaght now and up as far as Jobstown, mountain country. I got a call from a girl who lived up there who was related to another girl who was helping us with the search. Well she was convinced that Goldie was running around with a pack of dogs up there. Her very own gang, what. I was back to work full time and hadn't got much time so at lunchtime I'd get the Luas up a few days a week and look about the place. This was a needle in a haystack stuff again. She was even seen around Ballybowden Industrial Estate. She gets around alright.

This went on through November. The last day I was up there I went up as far as saggart and down the Blessington Road and I said "I tell ya, if she gets onto this road and crosses it she's heading down the country, down to Wicklow and Wexford – or via Saggart and then it's Kildare. I have a few cousins in Kildare so I could ask them to keep an eye out. This was tough, I just didn't have enough time to be cycling to Kildare.

A man rang and said he seen her in an industrial estate in City West so I went there and that was the last time we would hear anything about Goldie on that side of Christmas.

I started saying to myself then that's it she is gone down the country. All we could do was inform vets all around the country and that was taken care off from one of the girls who was already linked to all of them. It got really quiet on the

Goldie front I didn't hear a thing. I was convinced now that someone either had her or she was running around Wicklow. I even thought she was dead.

So Christmas had come and the only hint of a sighting was a the girl from Jobstown who said she was convinced she saw Goldie running around Jobstown. If she could get a picture of the dog she had seen then we'd know for sure.

So we took a rest for the Christmas and I just kept an eye on Facebook and got on with the crimbo but it just wasn't the same without our Goldie. It was a sad Christmas.It was one of the warmest Christmas's I can remember, so that was a bonus. If she was out there at least it was warm.

Then just after Christmas I got a call to say Goldie was seen in the grounds of Tallaght Hospital, and would I go up there straight away and take a look. As soon as I got back to work one of the girls came by to drive us up to Tallaght Hospital. In the back of my head I was saying it's probably not, but sure we'll know soon enough. We drove in that first day and met up with the girl who had been spoting her. This girl was the niece of another person who had been in on this story from the start and had been out searching on and off for months looking for Goldie. She showed us where Goldie was hanging out which was in the bushes at the right side car park. If you were ever in Tallaght Hospital you would know what I mean. So we drove around for a bit and then as we pulled into the top car park there she was. I got a good look at her and I nearly jumped out of me skin. "That's Goldie, that's her" I shouted in my loudest voice of course frighting her and half the patients. She swiftly ran back into the bushes, but it was definatly her. My God what about that. So she heard my voice but didn't come. As I was told, she was in survival mode where she kind of temporarily forgot home and is just living to survive now. She had changed a bit. She had more fur on her as she'd been outside for six months now. And she looked healthy. Wow look at that. We were amazed. This dog had just walked from Finglas to Tallaght, the longest way possibleand here she was, Goldie, not a blemish on her.

The next day I met up with a man and his son from animal rescue who was working as a trapper. Now I don't mean one who traps animals for game, I mean one who traps them to save them. All types from cats and dogs to horses and birds, anything that's lost. He was going to set a couple of humane traps around the grounds of Tallaght Hospital and then we would take it in shifts to keep an eye out. They would be opened first thing in the morning and then closed again at night in case anything other than Goldie went into them. That was the plan. A few days I thought and we'd have her. But no, it was goin to take time, 5 weeks of time. I would do what I could mainly at lunchtime and the other guys would do the rest. Goldie kept her distance, she just came out at almost the same time just to get the food and then back out of sight. It was a waiting game. A stakeout, with plenty of stake for

Goldie. She had them wrapped around her paws at this stage, food coming from all angles. The staff, the hospital.visitors, and us. But that was fine she was emaciated at one stage so I didn't mind. It's mad when your own dog doesn't recognise you. People were saying just call her, or just go over and grab her, but that's not what you do. They were saying she will have to be rehabilitated to get her back to being a pet. Also she was small so we were not at her level. So it was a difficult situation to be in. We also needed to keep this information just between ourselves because there was huge interest in Goldie and we had to try keep it a secret and not say too much or we might have a situation where loads of people might come to the hospital and then security would have to scrap the whole thing. We kept taking photos from a distance and then analysing them later to make sure it was her. But it was her. I knew it was. Unless of course she had a twin? It was very possible she could have as she was from a litter of 9. But what were the chances of that. This went on and on and on days into days and weeks into weeks. We were gaining her trust and getting closer all the time. She was crafty though,she figured out how to remove the food from the trap without getting caught. She was like the bear in the advert that when your back is turned she was making faces and laughing behind your back. I remember the cold at this time,how cold it was some of the nights out there in the carpark. Where was she staying to keep warm? Even when it rained she came out dry. A tunnel, a hole or somebodies back garden maybe? Somewhere there's food no doubt. We sat out a few afternoons chatting in the car waiting and I can tell you, you have to have heaps of patients for this kind of thing. Fair play to those who do this all the time, it is a labour of love that's for sure. And thank God for them. I got a good dose at this time, not the old man flu, but a good old laid up in bed dose that lasted a week or so. I could view progress from my phone. That's another area where the old moby comes in handy. Communication makes it all the more easy nowadays than the old days.

Here is an outline of the distance she covered, I'm not sure of the absolute direction but this will be accurate enough:

Clancy Avenue, Finglas; Jamestown Road; Jamestown Industrial Estate; Superquinn, Clune Road; Glasnevin Avenue; Ballymun Road; DCU; Collins Avenue, Whitehall; Collins Avenue again. Now she was sen all over these areas including Artane. I remember that one well; Artane in the rain. From Beaumont to Gracepark Road and into Sion Hill; Glandore Road; Annadale Drive; Phibsboro Avenue; Griffith Downs. We know she slept here for a while and the Convalescent Hospital; Shalmartin Road, Brian Road; Marino; Fairview; Fairview Park; over the train tracks and on down into Lidl at East Wall; all around the Industrial Estates around East Wall; Sherrif Street; The 3 Arena; she crossed the road, God alone knows how, and on into Dublin Port. She spent 2 weeks here then went over the Eastlink Bridge to Ringsend; Ringsend

Park no doubt; all around Stella Gardens; Barrow Street and then she cottoned on to the Dodder, which I'd say she scooted across to Ballsbridge; Ranelagh, Rathmines; Terenure; Orwell Road; Milltown, Dropping Well; up to Bushy Park; Tesco Rathfarnham; up and down for days. Then she somehow ended up getting onto Kimmage Road and marched all the way to Perrystown; back down again and ended on DCaptains Road; all the way down to Poddle Park; Captains Road; Bangor Road; Stanaway Road; Sundrive Road; Clareville and back to Terenure; Bushy Park. Eventually she headed back to Perrystown; Whitehall Road; Likeklin and into Tymon Park where she followed the river to Speakers Connolly and into Firhouse. She kept reverting back to Rathfarnham and back up to Firhouse; Old Bawn and Old Mill Bar. Then it was Jobstown, Tallaght and all the surrounding areas. She even ended up in Ballymount Industrial Estate, eventually heading up to Citywest; Fortunestown and eventually coming to rest in Tallaght Hospital. Phew! There are so many other roads she visited but I'll let you remember those.

I always remember getting a lift one night from Tallaght Hospital and the journey only took 15 or 20mins on the M50. That's all, 20mins to get from Tallaght to Finglas in a car. It took Goldie 8 months to get to Tallaght Hospital from Finglas, the longest way possible. I have seen how people came together all through her journey in every place she visited somebody came out night and day and helped. I have seen how a Facebook page can grow from one or two people at the beginning to over a thousand people and it's still working today to help other dogs find their way back home.

Then one Wednesday we arrived at Tallaght Hospital at lunchtime and it was a really nice day. The weather had been very bad up till now and it was keeping her away. There was no sign of her. So I walked up to The Square, did a few laps and headed back down to the hospital. I was walking out the door when I saw 2 girls looking at the poster that I had put on the poles a while back. I said to myself yes if only you knew the chase she put on for us, imagine if we got her today imagine. I remember listening to walls came tumbling down by Paul Weller, a great song, mad how that sticks in your head. I walked into the car park and I could see her in the distance up on the hill. As I drew closer I could see her looking at me, like really looking, so I put out my hands and made a few gestures that I always made at her, I said "there you are Goldie there you are. How have you been? Are you coming home with me Goldie"? Next thing I knew she was sliding down the hill really slowly like, not too sure but getting closer all the time. I turned around and realised I was on me own so I had to play me cards right, (she was in a submissive position I found out later), so I kept talking to her, then she ran back in so I walked away a bit, then I turned back and she was looking over the wall like saying "hey where are you goin"? So I slowly walked back and a girl who was watching said is that dog is that dog, I said "yes, hold on for a minute" as she was taking pictures on her phone while I was trying to get a grip on Goldie without scaring her. Just then she ran back up the hill and then out into the car park, as if all the tension and uncertainty fell away from her. She let out a bark and bounced up into my arms. She licked the face off me and I had to fight the tears back. Then lots of people started walking by saying they got her they got the dog. I struggled to get the lead that was in my pocket for months to get it around her neck, and only then I knew she was safe. I phoned the man from animal rescue who was on his way back to do his stint. We got her I shouted we got Goldie. We got her into the car and drove out of the hospital for the first time and I said "Goldie,were goin home". She sat up on my lap to look out the window she knew it was me and you could feel her shaking with excitement. We drove down to meet the girl, who without, I don't think we would have got this result. As we pulled into her job she was beside herself with happiness because it had been a success, it all paid off.

After that we drove through the Phoenix Park to Finglas, She hadn't been here in months.

We arrived home and she knew straight away where she was. She went straight to the garden and ran up and down with James her best buddy.

She came out of her ordeal unscathed except for a few bumps from the briars and bushes, but that was all. She had run a marathon and walked some distance but she was home now safe and happy and it was over, her odyssey was complete.

We got a call from a local paper in Tallaght Shopping Centre to do a little story on her which we agreed of course. So that went down well. It was a lovely little piece to boost it all up. She was famous now that she was saved.

It's eight months now since we got her back and I've just come to the end of her story. But it doesn't end here of course. Goldie is doin great. Back to her old self just like I was told, out of survival and into I don't want to go out anymore mode, (which I didn't want to allow). So I bought her a nice harness and brought her out with her pal James, which I want to tell you, is a completely different character, more puppy like Goldie, hey what happened to that athletic Goldie. Up all night Goldie taking chase around housing estates, surprising taxi men and general strangers alike. Well, wait till I tell you.

The other day there we were me, James and Golders. If you can remember there was a picture of her just her behind, running sideways like, trotting off along a lane in Perrystown. Well it was a nice evening just about getting dark kind of an evening when all of a sudden I looked down and there was one empty harness and I looked and there she was trotting away again. "OH NO" I said and I took off after her calling her GOLDIE,GOLDIE, with James in tow. A couple of kids watching as she breezed on by laughing at my panic of course. Please don't cross the road go on go on left yes left quick to the right and then she disappeared into her front garden and waited as I walked in catching my breath and sighing with relief it worked this time she ran right the way she had been walking home, home, home, a scratch on the door and in to her spot for a lovely safe sleep.

As I lay in my own bed that night I wondered if she had of ran again would she run the same way? would she have the energy? I think she would. But really when you think of it Goldie' s story happens every day all over the world and there are those who spring into action to come to their rescue and never let up to save our loyal and trusted and sometimes wild little pals. This was a journey I will never forget as long as I live. When asked would I do it again? Yes indeed. Because we love our animals and they love us back and that's all that matters.

So the next time you see a little dog, cat, horse, whatever in distress take out your phone, take a picture and post it on the many sites that are on Facebook and even upload it onto the find Goldie site and give them all the chance of getting found and brought home safe because we are their only hope.

THE END

Lightning Source UK Ltd.
Milton Keynes UK
UKHW010617171019
351778UK00001B/246/P

9 781543 494136